MW00454079

RUTH - ONE WOMAN'S JOURNEY FROM LOSS TO LEGACY

Copyright © 2017 by Love God Greatly Ministry

Permission is granted to print and reproduce this document for the purpose of completing the *Ruth - One Woman's Journey from Loss to Legacy* online Bible study. Please do not alter this document in any way. All rights reserved.

Published in Dallas by Love God Greatly.

Coloring artwork designed by Rachel Brosnahan. All rights reserved.

Unless otherwise noted, Scripture quotations are taken from *The Holy Bible, English Standard Version* Copyright © 2001 by Crossway Bibles, a publishing ministry of Good News Publishers.

Printed in the United States of America

Library of Congress Cataloging-in-Publication Data

Printed in the United States of America

22 21 20 19 18 17
6   5   4   3   2   1

Contents

Welcome

WE ARE GLAD you have decided to join us in this Bible study! First of all, please know that you have been prayed for! It is not a coincidence you are participating in this study.

Our prayer for you is simple: that you will grow closer to our Lord as you dig into His Word each and every day! As you develop the discipline of being in God's Word on a daily basis, our prayer is that you will fall in love with Him even more as you spend time reading from the Bible.

Each day before you read the assigned scripture(s), pray and ask God to help you understand it. Invite Him to speak to you through His Word. Then listen. It's His job to speak to you, and it's your job to listen and obey.

Take time to read the verses over and over again. We are told in Proverbs to search and you will find: "Search for it like silver, and hunt for it like hidden treasure. Then you will understand" (Prov. 2:4–5 NCV).

We are thrilled to provide these different resources for you as you participate in our online Bible study:

- *Ruth - One Woman's Journey from Loss to Legacy* Study Journal
- Reading Plan
- Weekly Blog Posts (Mondays, Wednesdays, and Fridays)
- Weekly Memory Verses
- Weekly Monday Videos
- Weekly Challenges
- Online Community: Facebook, Twitter, Instagram, LoveGodGreatly.com
- Hashtags: #LoveGodGreatly

All of us here at Love God Greatly can't wait for you to get started, and we hope to see you at the finish line. Endure, persevere, press on—and don't give up! Finish well what you are beginning today. We will be here every step of the way, cheering you on! We are in this together. Fight to rise early, to push back the stress of the day, to sit alone and spend time in God's Word! Let's see what God has in store for you in this study! Journey with us as we learn to love God greatly with our lives!

Our Community

LOVE GOD GREATLY (LGG) is a beautiful community of women who use a variety of technology platforms to keep each other accountable in God's Word.

We start with a simple Bible reading plan, but it doesn't stop there.

Some women gather in homes and churches locally, while others connect online with women across the globe. Whatever the method, we lovingly lock arms and unite for this purpose: to love God greatly with our lives.

In today's fast-paced technology-driven world, it would be easy to study God's Word in an isolated environment that lacks encouragement or support, but that isn't the intention here at Love God Greatly. God created us to live in community with Him and with those around us.

We need each other, and we live life better together.

Because of this, would you consider reaching out and doing this study with someone?

All of us have women in our lives who need friendship, accountability, and have the desire to dive into God's Word on a deeper level. Rest assured we'll be studying right alongside you—learning with you, cheering for you, enjoying sweet fellowship, and smiling from ear to ear as we watch God unite women together—intentionally connecting hearts and minds for His glory.

It's pretty unreal, this opportunity we have to grow not only closer to God through this study but also to each other. So here's the challenge: call your mom, your sister, your grandma, the girl across the street, or the college friend across the country. Gather a group of girls from your church or workplace, or meet in a coffee shop with friends you have always wished you knew better. Utilize the beauty of connecting online for inspiration and accountability, and take opportunities to meet in person when you can.

Arm-in-arm and hand-in-hand, let's do this thing...together.

How to SOAP

WE'RE PROUD OF YOU.

We really want you to know that.

We're proud of you for making the commitment to be in God's Word, to be reading it each day and applying it to your life, the beautiful life our Lord has given you.

In this study we offer you a study journal to accompany the verses we are reading. This journal is designed to help you interact with God's Word and learn to dig deeper, encouraging you to slow down and reflect on what God is saying to you that day.

At Love God Greatly, we use the SOAP Bible study method. Before beginning, let's take a moment to define this method and share why we recommend using it during your quiet time.

Why SOAP It?

It's one thing to simply read Scripture. But when you interact with it, intentionally slowing down to really reflect on it, suddenly words start popping off the page. The SOAP method allows you to dig deeper into Scripture and see more than you would if you simply read the verses and then went on your merry way. Please take the time to SOAP through our Bible studies and see for yourself how much more you get from your daily reading. You'll be amazed.

What Does SOAP Mean?

S stands for **Scripture**. Physically write out the verses. You'll be amazed at what God will reveal to you just by taking the time to slow down and write out what you are reading!

O stands for **observation**. What do you see in the verses that you're reading? Who is the intended audience? Is there a repetition of words? What words stand out to you?

A stands for **application**. This is when God's Word becomes personal. What is God saying to you today? How can you apply what you just read to your own personal life? What changes do you need to make? Is there action you need to take?

P stands for **prayer**. Pray God's Word back to Him. Spend time thanking Him. If He has revealed something to you during this time in His Word, pray about it. If He has revealed some sin that is in your life, confess. And remember, He loves you dearly.

Follow This Example

Scripture: Read and write out Colossians 1:5–8.

> "The faith and love that spring from the hope stored up for you in heaven and about which you have already heard in the true message of the gospel that has come to you. In the same way, the gospel is bearing fruit and growing throughout the whole world— just as it has been doing among you since the day you heard it and truly understood God's grace. You learned it from Epaphras, our dear fellow servant, who is a faithful minister of Christ on our behalf, and who also told us of your love in the Spirit" (NIV).

Observation: Write what stands out to you.

> When you combine faith and love, you get hope. We must remember that our hope is in heaven; it is yet to come. The gospel is the Word of truth. The gospel is continually bearing fruit and growing from the first day to the last. It just takes one person to change a whole community…Epaphras.

Application: Apply this scripture to your own life.

> God used one man, Epaphras, to change a whole town. I was reminded that we are simply called to tell others about Christ; it's God's job to spread the gospel, to grow it, and have it bear fruit. I felt today's verses were almost directly spoken to Love God Greatly women: "The gospel is bearing fruit and growing throughout the whole world—just as it has been doing among you since the day you heard it and truly understood God's grace."

It's so fun when God's Word comes alive and encourages us in our current situation! My passionate desire is that all the women involved in our LGG Bible study will understand God's grace and have a thirst for His Word. I was moved by this quote from my Bible commentary today: "God's Word is not just for our information, it is for our transformation."

Prayer: Pray over this.

> Dear Lord, please help me to be an "Epaphras," to tell others about You and then leave the results in Your loving hands. Please help me to understand and apply personally what I have read today to my life, thereby becoming more and more like You each and every day. Help me to live a life that bears the fruit of faith and love, anchoring my hope in heaven, not here on earth. Help me to remember that the best is yet to come!

SOAP It Up

Remember, the most important ingredients in the SOAP method are your interaction with God's Word and your application of His Word to your life:

> Blessed is the one who does not walk in step with the wicked or stand in the way that sinners take or sit in the company of mockers, but whose delight is in the law of the LORD, and who meditates on his law day and night. That person is like a tree planted by streams of water, which yields its fruit in season and whose leaf does not wither—whatever they do prospers. (Ps. 1:1–3, NIV)

Reading Plan

WEEK 1

Monday	Read: Ruth 1:1-3; Leviticus 26:1-4,18-20	Soap: Ruth 1:1-3
Tuesday	Read: Ruth 1:4-5; Genesis 19:30	Soap: Ruth 1:4-5
Wednesday	Read: Ruth 1:6-14	Soap: Ruth 1:8
Thursday	Read: Ruth 1:15-18; Proverbs 31:25	Soap: Ruth 1:16,17
Friday	Read: Ruth 1:19-22; 1 Peter 4:19; Psalm 34:19	Soap: Ruth 1:19-21
Response Day		

WEEK 2

Monday	Read: Ruth 2:1-3; Proverbs 20:24	Soap: Ruth 2:3
Tuesday	Read: Ruth 2:4-7; Leviticus 19:9-10	Soap: Ruth 2:7
Wednesday	Read: Ruth 2:8-13; Psalm 57:1	Soap: Ruth 2:11-12
Thursday	Read: Ruth 2:14-17; Psalm 34:10	Soap: Ruth 2:17
Friday	Read: Ruth 2:18-23; Psalm 119:68	Soap: Ruth 2:20
Response Day		

WEEK 3

Monday	Read: Ruth 3:1-5	Soap: Ruth 3:3-4
Tuesday	Read: Ruth 3:6-9	Soap: Ruth 3:8-9
Wednesday	Read: Ruth 3:10-11; Proverbs 31:31	Soap: Ruth 3:11
Thursday	Read: Ruth 3:12-13	Soap: Ruth 3:12-13
Friday	Read: Ruth 3:14-18; 1 Thessalonians 4:3-4	Soap: Ruth 3:14-15
Response Day		

WEEK 4

Monday	Read: Ruth 4:1-6	Soap: Ruth 5:5-6
Tuesday	Read: Ruth 4:7-10	Soap: Ruth 4:9-10
Wednesday	Read: Ruth 4:11-12; Genesis 29:31; Gen. 30:22	Soap: Ruth 4:11-12
Thursday	Read: Ruth 4:13-16, Psalm 30:11	Soap: Ruth 4:14-15, Psalm 30:11
Friday	Read: Ruth 4:17-22; Matthew 1:1,21	Soap: Ruth 4:17; Matthew 1:21
Response Day		

Goals

WE BELIEVE it's important to write out goals for this study. Take some time now and write three goals you would like to focus on as you begin to rise each day and dig into God's Word. Make sure and refer back to these goals throughout the next four weeks to help you stay focused. You can do it!

My goals are:

1.

2.

3.

Signature: _____

Date: _____

Introduction

WE ARE VERY EXCITED to be studying the book of Ruth with you.

Ruth takes place during the time of the Judges, and as we begin reading we see the curtain lift on a scene of tragedy. Naomi, who had already lost her husband, now mourns the loss of both of her sons.

As Naomi makes the hard decision to leave the home she shared with her husband and children and go back to the land where she was raised, Orpah, her daugher in-law, decides to return to her family in the land of Moab. More loss.

But then we meet Ruth. Ruth is also a Moabite woman, but it is evident that she has come to accept the one true God as her own God (Ruth 1:16). With this love for the Lord comes a love for and devotion to Naomi that causes her to pledge her life to her. Together these two widows travel to Naomi's hometown of Bethlehem.

While Ruth is a story of loss and heartache, we also see mourning turn to dancing. We see women who are alone and destitute find love and acceptance. We will see themes of loyalty, kindness, boldness, love, and redemption. **But ultimately, Ruth is a book about the providence of God.** While these two ladies travelled with utter sadness and fear of the unknown towards Bethlehem, they did not realize that God was leading them to a place of hope and redemption.

In the book of Ruth we see Romans 8:28 come to life:

And we know that for those who love God
all things work together for good,
for those who are called according to His purpose.

In Ruth we see God take ordinary people through painful events to manifest His glory and bring about their good. We should never underestimate the seemingly small events in our lives. Whether it is caring for family, getting married, working, showing kindness to our neighbors, or raising children... all of it is being used by God for the good of those who love Him, for His glory, and for the salvation of others.

No event or person is insignificant in the plan of God. This study should fill us with great hope as we see every event and person sovereignly placed in God's beautiful patchwork, whose final piece will be the return of Christ Himself.

Looking to Jesus,

Jen

Week 1

Week 1 Challenge (Note: You can find this listed in our Monday blog post):

Prayer focus for this week: Spend time praying for your family members.

	Praying	Praise
Monday		
Tuesday		
Wednesday		
Thursday		
Friday		

For where you go I will go,
and where you lodge I will lodge.
Your people shall be my people,
and your God my God.

RUTH 1:16

Scripture for Week 1

MONDAY

RUTH 1:1-3

[1] In the days when the judges ruled there was a famine in the land, and a man of Bethlehem in Judah went to sojourn in the country of Moab, he and his wife and his two sons. [2] The name of the man was Elimelech and the name of his wife Naomi, and the names of his two sons were Mahlon and Chilion. They were Ephrathites from Bethlehem in Judah. They went into the country of Moab and remained there. [3] But Elimelech, the husband of Naomi, died, and she was left with her two sons.

LEVITICUS 26:1-4

[1] "You shall not make idols for yourselves or erect an image or pillar, and you shall not set up a figured stone in your land to bow down to it, for I am the Lord your God. [2] You shall keep my Sabbaths and reverence my sanctuary: I am the Lord.

[3] "If you walk in my statutes and observe my commandments and do them, [4] then I will give you your rains in their season, and the land shall yield its increase, and the trees of the field shall yield their fruit.

LEVITICUS 26:18-20

[18] And if in spite of this you will not listen to me, then I will discipline you again sevenfold for your sins, [19] and I will break the pride of your power, and I will make your heavens like iron and your earth like bronze. [20] And your strength shall be spent in vain, for your land shall not yield its increase, and the trees of the land shall not yield their fruit.

TUESDAY

RUTH 1:4-5

[4] These took Moabite wives; the name of the one was Orpah and the name of the other Ruth. They lived there about ten years, [5] and both

Mahlon and Chilion died, so that the woman was left without her two sons and her husband.

GENESIS 19:30

[30] Now Lot went up out of Zoar and lived in the hills with his two daughters, for he was afraid to live in Zoar. So he lived in a cave with his two daughters.

WEDNESDAY

RUTH 1:6-14

[6] Then she arose with her daughters-in-law to return from the country of Moab, for she had heard in the fields of Moab that the Lord had visited his people and given them food. [7] So she set out from the place where she was with her two daughters-in-law, and they went on the way to return to the land of Judah. [8] But Naomi said to her two daughters-in-law, "Go, return each of you to her mother's house. May the Lord deal kindly with you, as you have dealt with the dead and with me. [9] The Lord grant that you may find rest, each of you in the house of her husband!" Then she kissed them, and they lifted up their voices and wept. [10] And they said to her, "No, we will return with you to your people." [11] But Naomi said, "Turn back, my daughters; why will you go with me? Have I yet sons in my womb that they may become your husbands? [12] Turn back, my daughters; go your way, for I am too old to have a husband. If I should say I have hope, even if I should have a husband this night and should bear sons, [13] would you therefore wait till they were grown? Would you therefore refrain from marrying? No, my daughters, for it is exceedingly bitter to me for your sake that the hand of the Lord has gone out against me."[14] Then they lifted up their voices and wept again. And Orpah kissed her mother-in-law, but Ruth clung to her.

THURSDAY

RUTH 1:15-18

[15] And she said, "See, your sister-in-law has gone back to her people

and to her gods; return after your sister-in-law." ¹⁶ But Ruth said, "Do not urge me to leave you or to return from following you. For where you go I will go, and where you lodge I will lodge. Your people shall be my people, and your God my God.¹⁷ Where you die I will die, and there will I be buried. May the Lord do so to me and more also if anything but death parts me from you." ¹⁸ And when Naomi saw that she was determined to go with her, she said no more.

PROVERBS 31:25

²⁵ Strength and dignity are her clothing,

and she laughs at the time to come.

FRIDAY

RUTH 1:19-22

¹⁹ So the two of them went on until they came to Bethlehem. And when they came to Bethlehem, the whole town was stirred because of them. And the women said, "Is this Naomi?" ²⁰ She said to them, "Do not call me Naomi; call me Mara, for the Almighty has dealt very bitterly with me. ²¹ I went away full, and the Lord has brought me back empty. Why call me Naomi, when the Lord has testified against me and the Almighty has brought calamity upon me?"

²² So Naomi returned, and Ruth the Moabite her daughter-in-law with her, who returned from the country of Moab. And they came to Bethlehem at the beginning of barley harvest.

1PETER 4:19

¹⁹ Therefore let those who suffer according to God's will entrust their souls to a faithful Creator while doing good.

PSALM 34:19

¹⁹ Many are the afflictions of the righteous,

but the Lord delivers him out of them all.

Monday

READ: Ruth 1:1-3; Leviticus 26:1-4,18-20

SOAP: Ruth 1:1-3

Scripture - Write out the **Scripture** passage for the day.

Observations - Write down 1 or 2 **observations** from the passage.

Monday

Applications - Write down 1 or 2 **applications** from the passage.

Pray - Write out a **prayer** over what you learned from today's passage.

-Visit our website today for the corresponding blog post!-

Tuesday

READ: Ruth 1:4-5; Genesis 19:30
SOAP: Ruth 1:4-5

Scripture - Write out the **Scripture** passage for the day.

Observations - Write down 1 or 2 **observations** from the passage.

Tuesday

Applications - Write down 1 or 2 **applications** from the passage.

Pray - Write out a **prayer** over what you learned from today's passage.

Wednesday

READ: Ruth 1:6-14
SOAP: Ruth 1:8

Scripture - Write out the **Scripture** passage for the day.

Observations - Write down 1 or 2 **observations** from the passage.

Wednesday

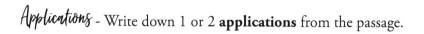

Applications - Write down 1 or 2 **applications** from the passage.

Pray - Write out a **prayer** over what you learned from today's passage.

-Visit our website today for the corresponding blog post!-

Thursday

READ: Ruth 1:15-18; Proverbs 31:25
SOAP: Ruth 1:16,17

Scripture - Write out the **Scripture** passage for the day.

Observations - Write down 1 or 2 **observations** from the passage.

Thursday

Applications - Write down 1 or 2 **applications** from the passage.

Pray - Write out a **prayer** over what you learned from today's passage.

Friday

READ: Ruth 1:19-22; 1 Peter 4:19; Psalm 34:19
SOAP: Ruth 1:19-21

Scripture - Write out the **Scripture** passage for the day.

Observations - Write down 1 or 2 **observations** from the passage.

Friday

Applications - Write down 1 or 2 **applications** from the passage.

Pray - Write out a **prayer** over what you learned from today's passage.

-Visit our website today for the corresponding blog post!-

Reflection Questions

1. Why do you think Orpah returns to Moab instead of following Ruth and Naomi?

2. Why did Naomi want to change her name to Mara?

3. Why does Naomi say that God has "brought calamity" on her?

4. Do you think Naomi is trusting God or distrusting him?

5. How does the city to which they returned (Bethlehem) become significant in the subsequent Bible story?

My Response

Week 2

Week 2 Challenge (Note: You can find this listed in our Monday blog post):

Prayer focus for this week: Spend time praying for your country.

	Praying	Praise
Monday		
Tuesday		
Wednesday		
Thursday		
Friday		

The Lord repay you
for what you have done,
and a full reward be given you
by the Lord, the God of Israel,
under whose wings you have
come to take refuge!

RUTH 2:12

Scripture for Week 2

MONDAY

RUTH 2:1-3

[1] Now Naomi had a relative of her husband's, a worthy man of the clan of Elimelech, whose name was Boaz. [2] And Ruth the Moabite said to Naomi, "Let me go to the field and glean among the ears of grain after him in whose sight I shall find favor." And she said to her, "Go, my daughter." [3] So she set out and went and gleaned in the field after the reapers, and she happened to come to the part of the field belonging to Boaz, who was of the clan of Elimelech.

PROVERBS 20:24

[24] A man's steps are from the Lord;

how then can man understand his way?

TUESDAY

RUTH 2:4-7

[4] And behold, Boaz came from Bethlehem. And he said to the reapers, "The Lord be with you!" And they answered, "The Lord bless you." [5] Then Boaz said to his young man who was in charge of the reapers, "Whose young woman is this?"[6] And the servant who was in charge of the reapers answered, "She is the young Moabite woman, who came back with Naomi from the country of Moab. [7] She said, 'Please let me glean and gather among the sheaves after the reapers.' So she came, and she has continued from early morning until now, except for a short rest."

LEVITICUS 19:9-10

[9] "When you reap the harvest of your land, you shall not reap your field right up to its edge, neither shall you gather the gleanings after your harvest. [10] And you shall not strip your vineyard bare, neither shall you gather the fallen grapes of your vineyard. You shall leave them for the poor and for the sojourner: I am the Lord your God.

WEDNESDAY

RUTH 2:8-13

8 Then Boaz said to Ruth, "Now, listen, my daughter, do not go to glean in another field or leave this one, but keep close to my young women. 9 Let your eyes be on the field that they are reaping, and go after them. Have I not charged the young men not to touch you? And when you are thirsty, go to the vessels and drink what the young men have drawn." 10 Then she fell on her face, bowing to the ground, and said to him, "Why have I found favor in your eyes, that you should take notice of me, since I am a foreigner?" 11 But Boaz answered her, "All that you have done for your mother-in-law since the death of your husband has been fully told to me, and how you left your father and mother and your native land and came to a people that you did not know before. 12 The Lord repay you for what you have done, and a full reward be given you by the Lord, the God of Israel, under whose wings you have come to take refuge!" 13 Then she said, "I have found favor in your eyes, my lord, for you have comforted me and spoken kindly to your servant, though I am not one of your servants."

PSALM 57:1

1 Be merciful to me, O God, be merciful to me,

for in you my soul takes refuge;

in the shadow of your wings I will take refuge,

till the storms of destruction pass by.

THURSDAY

RUTH 2:14-17

14 And at mealtime Boaz said to her, "Come here and eat some bread and dip your morsel in the wine." So she sat beside the reapers, and he passed to her roasted grain. And she ate until she was satisfied, and she had some left over. 15 When she rose to glean, Boaz instructed his young men, saying, "Let her glean even among the

sheaves, and do not reproach her. [16] And also pull out some from the bundles for her and leave it for her to glean, and do not rebuke her."

[17] So she gleaned in the field until evening. Then she beat out what she had gleaned, and it was about an ephah of barley.

PSALM 34:10

[10] The young lions suffer want and hunger;

but those who seek the Lord lack no good thing.

FRIDAY

RUTH 2:18-23

[18] And she took it up and went into the city. Her mother-in-law saw what she had gleaned. She also brought out and gave her what food she had left over after being satisfied. [19] And her mother-in-law said to her, "Where did you glean today? And where have you worked? Blessed be the man who took notice of you." So she told her mother-in-law with whom she had worked and said, "The man's name with whom I worked today is Boaz." [20] And Naomi said to her daughter-in-law, "May he be blessed by the Lord, whose kindness has not forsaken the living or the dead!" Naomi also said to her, "The man is a close relative of ours, one of our redeemers." [21] And Ruth the Moabite said, "Besides, he said to me, 'You shall keep close by my young men until they have finished all my harvest.'" [22] And Naomi said to Ruth, her daughter-in-law, "It is good, my daughter, that you go out with his young women, lest in another field you be assaulted." [23] So she kept close to the young women of Boaz, gleaning until the end of the barley and wheat harvests. And she lived with her mother-in-law.

PSALM 119:68

[68] You are good and do good;

teach me your statutes.

Monday

READ: Ruth 2:1-3; Proverbs 20:24
SOAP: Ruth 2:3

Scripture - Write out the **Scripture** passage for the day.

Observations - Write down 1 or 2 **observations** from the passage.

Monday

Applications - Write down 1 or 2 **applications** from the passage.

Pray - Write out a **prayer** over what you learned from today's passage.

-Visit our website today for the corresponding blog post!-

Tuesday

READ: Ruth 2:4-7; Leviticus 19:9-10

SOAP: Ruth 2:7

Scripture - Write out the **Scripture** passage for the day.

Observations - Write down 1 or 2 **observations** from the passage.

Tuesday

Applications - Write down 1 or 2 **applications** from the passage.

Pray - Write out a **prayer** over what you learned from today's passage.

Wednesday

READ: Ruth 2:8-13; Psalm 57:1
SOAP: Ruth 2:11-12

Scripture - Write out the **Scripture** passage for the day.

Observations - Write down 1 or 2 **observations** from the passage.

Wednesday

Applications - Write down 1 or 2 **applications** from the passage.

Pray - Write out a **prayer** over what you learned from today's passage.

-Visit our website today for the corresponding blog post!-

Thursday

READ: Ruth 2:14-17; Psalm 34:10
SOAP: Ruth 2:17

Scripture - Write out the **Scripture** passage for the day.

Observations - Write down 1 or 2 **observations** from the passage.

Thursday

Applications - Write down 1 or 2 **applications** from the passage.

Pray - Write out a **prayer** over what you learned from today's passage.

Friday

READ: Ruth 2:18-23; Psalm 119:68

SOAP: Ruth 2:20

Scripture - Write out the **Scripture** passage for the day.

Observations - Write down 1 or 2 **observations** from the passage.

Friday

Applications - Write down 1 or 2 **applications** from the passage.

Pray - Write out a **prayer** over what you learned from today's passage.

Reflection Questions

1. Ruth decides to go gleaning in Boaz's field. What does gleaning mean and what do we learn about Ruth's character?

2. What do verses 8-16 tell us about the kind of man Boaz was?

3. In verse 11, what specifically does Boaz notice about Ruth that makes him want to help her?

4. Naomi calls Boaz "one of our redeemers." What does she mean by this?

5. In Chapter 1 we see Naomi really struggling. Do you think verse 20 indicates a change in perspective and attitude? Why or why not?

My Response

Week 3

Week 3 Challenge (Note: You can find this listed in our Monday blog post):

Prayer focus for this week: Spend time praying for your friends.

Praying	Praise
Monday	
Tuesday	
Wednesday	
Thursday	
Friday	

Give her of the fruit of her hands, and let her works praise her in the gates.

PROVERBS 31:31

MONDAY

RUTH 3:1-5

[1] Then Naomi her mother-in-law said to her, "My daughter, should I not seek rest for you, that it may be well with you? [2] Is not Boaz our relative, with whose young women you were? See, he is winnowing barley tonight at the threshing floor.[3] Wash therefore and anoint yourself, and put on your cloak and go down to the threshing floor, but do not make yourself known to the man until he has finished eating and drinking. [4] But when he lies down, observe the place where he lies. Then go and uncover his feet and lie down, and he will tell you what to do." [5] And she replied, "All that you say I will do."

TUESDAY

RUTH 3:6-9

[6] So she went down to the threshing floor and did just as her mother-in-law had commanded her. [7] And when Boaz had eaten and drunk, and his heart was merry, he went to lie down at the end of the heap of grain. Then she came softly and uncovered his feet and lay down. [8] At midnight the man was startled and turned over, and behold, a woman lay at his feet! [9] He said, "Who are you?" And she answered, "I am Ruth, your servant. Spread your wings over your servant, for you are a redeemer."

WEDNESDAY

RUTH 3:10-11

[10] And he said, "May you be blessed by the Lord, my daughter. You have made this last kindness greater than the first in that you have not gone after young men, whether poor or rich. [11] And now, my daughter, do not fear. I will do for you all that you ask, for all my fellow townsmen know that you are a worthy woman.

PROVERBS 31:31

³¹ Give her of the fruit of her hands,

and let her works praise her in the gates.

THURSDAY

RUTH 3:12-13

¹² And now it is true that I am a redeemer. Yet there is a redeemer nearer than I.¹³ Remain tonight, and in the morning, if he will redeem you, good; let him do it. But if he is not willing to redeem you, then, as the Lord lives, I will redeem you. Lie down until the morning."

FRIDAY

RUTH 3:14-18

¹⁴ So she lay at his feet until the morning, but arose before one could recognize another. And he said, "Let it not be known that the woman came to the threshing floor." ¹⁵ And he said, "Bring the garment you are wearing and hold it out." So she held it, and he measured out six measures of barley and put it on her. Then she went into the city. ¹⁶ And when she came to her mother-in-law, she said, "How did you fare, my daughter?" Then she told her all that the man had done for her,¹⁷ saying, "These six measures of barley he gave to me, for he said to me, 'You must not go back empty-handed to your mother-in-law.'" ¹⁸ She replied, "Wait, my daughter, until you learn how the matter turns out, for the man will not rest but will settle the matter today."

1 THESSALONIANS 4:3-4

³ For this is the will of God, your sanctification: that you abstain from sexual immorality; ⁴ that each one of you know how to control his own body in holiness and honor

Monday

READ: Ruth 3:1-5
SOAP: Ruth 3:3-4

Scripture - Write out the **Scripture** passage for the day.

Observations - Write down 1 or 2 **observations** from the passage.

Monday

Applications - Write down 1 or 2 **applications** from the passage.

Pray - Write out a **prayer** over what you learned from today's passage.

-Visit our website today for the corresponding blog post!-

Tuesday

READ: Ruth 3:6-9

SOAP: Ruth 3:8-9

Scripture - Write out the **Scripture** passage for the day.

Observations - Write down 1 or 2 **observations** from the passage.

Tuesday

Applications - Write down 1 or 2 **applications** from the passage.

Pray - Write out a **prayer** over what you learned from today's passage.

Wednesday

READ: Ruth 3:10-11; Proverbs 31:31
SOAP: Ruth 3:11

Scripture - Write out the **Scripture** passage for the day.

Observations - Write down 1 or 2 **observations** from the passage.

Wednesday

Applications - Write down 1 or 2 **applications** from the passage.

Pray - Write out a **prayer** over what you learned from today's passage.

-Visit our website today for the corresponding blog post!-

Thursday

READ: Ruth 3:12-13
SOAP: Ruth 3:12-13

Scripture - Write out the **Scripture** passage for the day.

Observations - Write down 1 or 2 **observations** from the passage.

Thursday

Applications - Write down 1 or 2 **applications** from the passage.

Pray - Write out a **prayer** over what you learned from today's passage.

Friday

READ: Ruth 3:14-18; 1 Thessalonians 4:3-4

SOAP: Ruth 3:14-15

Scripture - Write out the **Scripture** passage for the day.

Observations - Write down 1 or 2 **observations** from the passage.

Friday

Applications - Write down 1 or 2 **applications** from the passage.

Pray - Write out a **prayer** over what you learned from today's passage.

-Visit our website today for the corresponding blog post!-

Reflection Questions

1. In verses 1-4 Naomi gives Ruth some strange instructions. What is Ruth supposed to do and what is the point of her actions?

2. What is Boaz's reaction to Ruth's request?

3. For some it may seem like the interaction between Ruth and Boaz was inappropriate. How would you explain what happened?

4. Why did Boaz first have to check with the other kinsman-redeemer?

5. Why did Boaz have Ruth stay until morning?

My Response

Week 4

Week 4 Challenge (Note: You can find this listed in our Monday blog post):

Prayer focus for this week: Spend time praying for your church.

	Praying	Praise
Monday		
Tuesday		
Wednesday		
Thursday		
Friday		

You have turned for me
my mourning into dancing;
you have loosed my sackcloth
and clothed me with gladness

PSALM 30:11

Scripture for Week 4

MONDAY

RUTH 4:1-6

[1] Now Boaz had gone up to the gate and sat down there. And behold, the redeemer, of whom Boaz had spoken, came by. So Boaz said, "Turn aside, friend; sit down here." And he turned aside and sat down. [2] And he took ten men of the elders of the city and said, "Sit down here." So they sat down. [3] Then he said to the redeemer, "Naomi, who has come back from the country of Moab, is selling the parcel of land that belonged to our relative Elimelech. [4] So I thought I would tell you of it and say, 'Buy it in the presence of those sitting here and in the presence of the elders of my people.' If you will redeem it, redeem it. But if you[a] will not, tell me, that I may know, for there is no one besides you to redeem it, and I come after you." And he said, "I will redeem it." [5] Then Boaz said, "The day you buy the field from the hand of Naomi, you also acquire Ruth[b] the Moabite, the widow of the dead, in order to perpetuate the name of the dead in his inheritance." [6] Then the redeemer said, "I cannot redeem it for myself, lest I impair my own inheritance. Take my right of redemption yourself, for I cannot redeem it."

TUESDAY

RUTH 4:7-10

[7] Now this was the custom in former times in Israel concerning redeeming and exchanging: to confirm a transaction, the one drew off his sandal and gave it to the other, and this was the manner of attesting in Israel. [8] So when the redeemer said to Boaz, "Buy it for yourself," he drew off his sandal. [9] Then Boaz said to the elders and all the people, "You are witnesses this day that I have bought from the hand of Naomi all that belonged to Elimelech and all that belonged to Chilion and to Mahlon. [10] Also Ruth the Moabite, the widow of Mahlon, I have bought to be my wife, to perpetuate the name of the dead in his inheritance, that the name of the dead may not be cut off from among his brothers and from the gate of his native place. You are witnesses this day."

WEDNESDAY

RUTH 4:11-12

¹¹ Then all the people who were at the gate and the elders said, "We are witnesses. May the Lord make the woman, who is coming into your house, like Rachel and Leah, who together built up the house of Israel. May you act worthily in Ephrathah and be renowned in Bethlehem, ¹² and may your house be like the house of Perez, whom Tamar bore to Judah, because of the offspring that the Lord will give you by this young woman."

GENESIS 29:31

³¹ When the Lord saw that Leah was hated, he opened her womb, but Rachel was barren.

GENESIS 30:22

²² Then God remembered Rachel, and God listened to her and opened her womb.

THURSDAY

RUTH 4:13-16

¹³ So Boaz took Ruth, and she became his wife. And he went in to her, and the Lord gave her conception, and she bore a son. ¹⁴ Then the women said to Naomi, "Blessed be the Lord, who has not left you this day without a redeemer, and may his name be renowned in Israel! ¹⁵ He shall be to you a restorer of life and a nourisher of your old age, for your daughter-in-law who loves you, who is more to you than seven sons, has given birth to him." ¹⁶ Then Naomi took the child and laid him on her lap and became his nurse.

PSALM 30:11

¹¹ You have turned for me my mourning into dancing;

you have loosed my sackcloth

and clothed me with gladness

FRIDAY

RUTH 4:17-22

[17] And the women of the neighborhood gave him a name, saying, "A son has been born to Naomi." They named him Obed. He was the father of Jesse, the father of David.

[18] Now these are the generations of Perez: Perez fathered Hezron, [19] Hezron fathered Ram, Ram fathered Amminadab, [20] Amminadab fathered Nahshon, Nahshon fathered Salmon, [21] Salmon fathered Boaz, Boaz fathered Obed, [22] Obed fathered Jesse, and Jesse fathered David.

MATTHEW 1:1

[1] The book of the genealogy of Jesus Christ, the son of David, the son of Abraham.

MATTHEW 1:21

[21] She will bear a son, and you shall call his name Jesus, for he will save his people from their sins.

Monday

READ: Ruth 4:1-6

SOAP: Ruth 5:5-6

Scripture - Write out the **Scripture** passage for the day.

Observations - Write down 1 or 2 **observations** from the passage.

Monday

Applications - Write down 1 or 2 **applications** from the passage.

Pray - Write out a **prayer** over what you learned from today's passage.

-Visit our website today for the corresponding blog post!-

Tuesday

READ: Ruth 4:7-10
SOAP: Ruth 4:9-10

Scripture - Write out the **Scripture** passage for the day.

Observations - Write down 1 or 2 **observations** from the passage.

Tuesday

Applications - Write down 1 or 2 **applications** from the passage.

Pray - Write out a **prayer** over what you learned from today's passage.

Wednesday

READ: Ruth 4:11-12; Genesis 29:31; Gen. 30:22
SOAP: Ruth 4:11-12

Scripture - Write out the **Scripture** passage for the day.

Observations - Write down 1 or 2 **observations** from the passage.

Wednesday

Applications - Write down 1 or 2 **applications** from the passage.

Pray - Write out a **prayer** over what you learned from today's passage.

-Visit our website today for the corresponding blog post!-

Thursday

READ: Ruth 4:13-16, Psalm 30:11
SOAP: Ruth 4:14-15, Psalm 30:11

Scripture - Write out the **Scripture** passage for the day.

Observations - Write down 1 or 2 **observations** from the passage.

Thursday

Applications - Write down 1 or 2 **applications** from the passage.

Pray - Write out a **prayer** over what you learned from today's passage.

Friday

READ: Ruth 4:17-22; Matthew 1:1,21
SOAP: Ruth 4:17; Matthew 1:21

Scripture - Write out the **Scripture** passage for the day.

Observations - Write down 1 or 2 **observations** from the passage.

Friday

Applications - Write down 1 or 2 **applications** from the passage.

Pray - Write out a **prayer** over what you learned from today's passage.

-Visit our website today for the corresponding blog post!-

Reflection Questions

1. Why did the man who was first in line to be Ruth's kinsman-redeemer turn it down?

2. What role did Obed play in the Biblical genealogy?

3. How is the story of Ruth a picture of Christ and His bride?

4. What do we learn about God in the book of Ruth?

5. What encouragements can you find from this book?

My Response

Know these truths from God's Word...

God loves you.

Even when you're feeling unworthy and like the world is stacked against you, God loves you - *yes, you* - and He has created you for great purpose.

> God's Word says, "God so loved the world that He gave His one and only Son, Jesus, that whoever believes in Him shall not perish, but have eternal life" (John 3:16).

Our sin separates us from God.

We are all sinners by nature and by choice, and because of this we are separated from God, who is holy.

> God's Word says, "All have sinned and fall short of the glory of God" (Romans 3:23).

Jesus died so that you might have life.

The consequence of sin is death, but your story doesn't have to end there! God's free gift of salvation is available to us because Jesus took the penalty for our sin when He died on the cross.

> God's Word says, "For the wages of sin is death, but the free gift of

God is eternal life in Christ Jesus our Lord" (Romans 6:23); "God demonstrates His own love toward us, in that while we were yet sinners, Christ died for us" (Romans 5:8).

Jesus lives!

Death could not hold Him, and three days after His body was placed in the tomb Jesus rose again, defeating sin and death forever! He lives today in heaven and is preparing a place in eternity for all who believe in Him.

God's Word says, "In my Father's house are many rooms. If it were not so, would I have told you that I go to prepare a place for you? And if I go and prepare a place for you, I will come again and will take you to myself, that where I am you may be also" (John 14:2-3).

Yes, you can KNOW that you are forgiven.

Accept Jesus as the only way to salvation…

Accepting Jesus as your Savior is not about what you can do, but rather about having faith in what Jesus has already done. It takes recognizing that you are a sinner, believing that Jesus died for your sins, and asking for forgiveness by placing your full trust in Jesus's work on the cross on your behalf.

God's Word says, "If you confess with your mouth that Jesus is Lord and believe in your heart that God raised him from the dead, you will be saved. For with the heart one believes and is justified, and with the mouth one confesses and is saved" (Romans 10:9-10).

Practically, what does that look like? With a sincere heart, you can pray a simple prayer like this:

God,

I know that I am a sinner.

I don't want to live another day without embracing

the love and forgiveness that You have for me.

I ask for Your forgiveness.

I believe that You died for my sins and rose from the dead.

I surrender all that I am and ask You to be Lord of my life.

Help me to turn from my sin and follow You.

Teach me what it means to walk in freedom as I live under Your grace,

and help me to grow in Your ways as I seek to know You more.

Amen.

If you just prayed this prayer (or something similar in your own words), would you email us at info@lovegodgreatly.com? We'd love to help get you started on this exciting journey as a child of God!

Welcome, friend. We're so glad you're here...

LOVE GOD GREATLY exists to inspire, encourage, and equip women all over the world to make God's Word a priority in their lives.

-INSPIRE-
women to make God's Word a priority in their daily lives through our Bible study resources.

-ENCOURAGE-
women in their daily walks with God through online community and personal accountability.

-EQUIP-
women to grow in their faith, so that they can effectively reach others for Christ.

Love God Greatly consists of a beautiful community of women who use a variety of technology platforms to keep each other accountable in God's Word.

We start with a simple Bible reading plan, but it doesn't stop there.

Some gather in homes and churches locally, while others connect online with women across the globe. Whatever the method, we lovingly lock arms and unite for this purpose...

to Love God Greatly with our lives.

At *Love God Greatly*, you'll find real, authentic women. Women who are imperfect, yet forgiven. Women who desire less of us, and a whole lot more of Jesus. Women who long to know God through his Word, because we know that Truth transforms and sets us free. ***Women who are better together, saturated in God's Word and in community with one another.***

Love God Greatly is a 501 (C) (3) non-profit organization. Funding for Love God Greatly comes through donations and proceeds from our online Bible study journals and books. LGG is committed to providing quality Bible study materials and believes finances should never get in the way of a woman being able to participate in one of our studies. All LGG journals and translated journals are available to download for free from LoveGodGreatly.com for those who cannot afford to purchase them. Our journals and books are also available for sale on Amazon. Search for "Love God Greatly" to see all of our Bible study journals and books. 100% of proceeds go directly back into supporting Love God Greatly and helping us inspire, encourage and equip women all over the world with God's Word.

THANK YOU for partnering with us!

What we offer:

18 + Translations | Bible Reading Plans | Online Bible Study
Love God Greatly App | 80 + Countries Served
Bible Study Journals & Books | Community Groups

Each Love God Greatly study includes:

Three Devotional Corresponding Blog Posts | Monday Vlog Videos
Memory Verses | Weekly Challenge | Weekly Reading Plan
Reflection Questions And More!

Other Love God Greatly studies include:

David | Ecclesiastes | Growing Through Prayer | Names Of God
Galatians | Psalm 119 | 1st & 2nd Peter | Made For Community | Esther
The Road To Christmas | The Source Of Gratitude | You Are Loved

YOU CAN FIND US ONLINE AT LOVEGODGREATLY.COM

63239392R00054

Made in the USA
Lexington, KY
01 May 2017